Scotland
from Space

Colin Baxter Photography, Grantown-on-Spey, Scotland

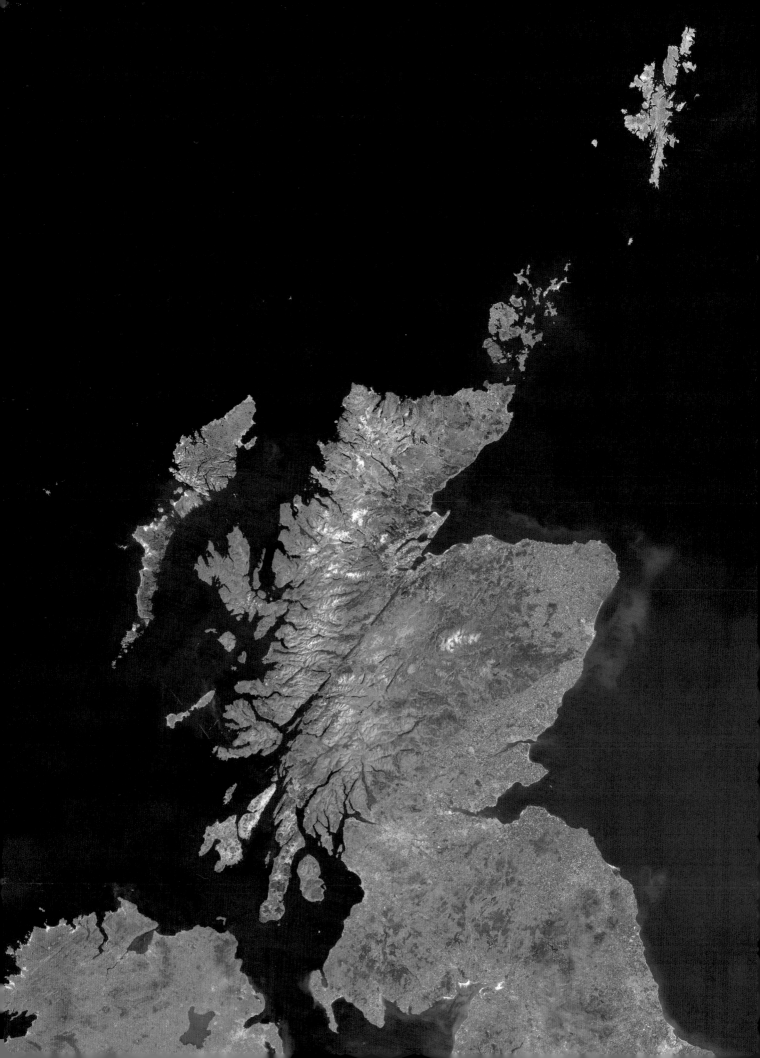

Scotland From Space

Scotland from space looks tiny – a mere speck on a slightly larger speck off the mighty continent of Europe. Yet that speck crams a great deal into its 7000-mile-long coastline – 30,000 square miles of ground, 30,000 freshwater lochs, 6600 rivers and 800 islands, as well as a population of 5 million people.

These fascinating images of Scotland were taken by NASA's Landsat-5 satellite. It orbits the earth at a height of 438 miles (705 km), at a speed of 16,777 mph (27,000 kph). This orbit is virtually polar and the satellite covers the world in 16 days, recording sequences of 71 mile (185 km) square scenes. To build up the coverage of a region or a whole country, several scenes have to be assembled, geometrically corrected, and then modified using state-of-the-art technology to show true colours.

From space we can pick out the key components that make Scotland what it is. A select few broad firths penetrate deep into the long North Sea coast, whilst long sinuous sea lochs pierce the western seaboard. Nowhere in Scotland is one more than 40 miles from the sea. Then there are the islands, hundreds of them, the majority hugging the west side. Most are no size at all, but from space the key ones are easily picked out – from the Firth of Clyde up through the Inner Hebrides, out across the Minch to the Western Isles, and north across the Pentland Firth to Orkney, Fair Isle and Shetland, the most northerly part of the British Isles. Inland, mountains and high hills are everywhere – including the Southern Uplands, which reach from Berwickshire in the east to Galloway in the southwest, and most spectacularly the Grampian Mountains which carpet most of the land north of the Forth-Clyde isthmus.

All else is predominately shades of green, depicting the lower-lying fertile ground that humans have tilled and tamed these past 10,000 years. And dotted about that green are areas of more intensive human settlement. From this great height we can just make out the cities of Aberdeen, Dundee, Edinburgh – and most noticeably the conurbation that is Glasgow. It is only as we descend from deepest space and come closer to the ground that the impact of humans on our landscape becomes more apparent. The patchwork-quilt fields emerge from the tapestry with a breathtaking clarity; so too the rooftops of farms and villages. Even individual streets in our cities and towns can be identified.

Scotland from space – as well as from Earth itself – is a truly fascinating sight.

◄ SCOTLAND FROM SPACE

This image of Scotland was taken by Landsat-5, a civilian observation satellite launched by NASA in 1984. It orbits the earth at a height of 438 miles (705 km), at a speed of 16,777 mph (27,000 kph), covering the earth every 16 days.

◀ FIRTH OF FORTH TO SOLWAY FIRTH

Edinburgh, North Berwick, Eyemouth and Berwick-upon-Tweed line the coast of the North Sea. In the southwest, beyond the undulating Borders hills, lies the Solway Firth.

▲ THE CITY OF EDINBURGH

The Forth Road and Rail Bridges link Edinburgh and the Lothians to southern Fife. The islands of Inchcolm, Inchkeith and Cramond stand guard in the Firth of Forth.

Scotland's land area of over 30,500 sq miles contains a population of 5.1 million people, 3.2 million of whom live in the 'central belt'. The total area of Scotland would fit into the USA almost 200 times.

▲ THE CITY OF GLASGOW

The River Clyde flows downstream from Motherwell and Hamilton to bisect Glasgow, and continues westward toward Dumbarton and the sea. East Kilbride, to the south of Glasgow, is surrounded by green fields.

▶ GLASGOW, AYRSHIRE, DUMFRIES & GALLOWAY, AND LANARKSHIRE

The southwest of Scotland – from the Ayrshire coast down to the Mull of Galloway, Scotland's most southerly point, eastward to Dumfries, and north again through Lanarkshire.

Scotland's prevailing winds arrive on Atlantic depressions from the southwest. The strongest high-level gust of wind recorded was on Cairn Gorm on 20 March, 1986 at 150 knots (172.6 mph) and the strongest low level gust at Fraserburgh of 123 knots (141.6 mph).

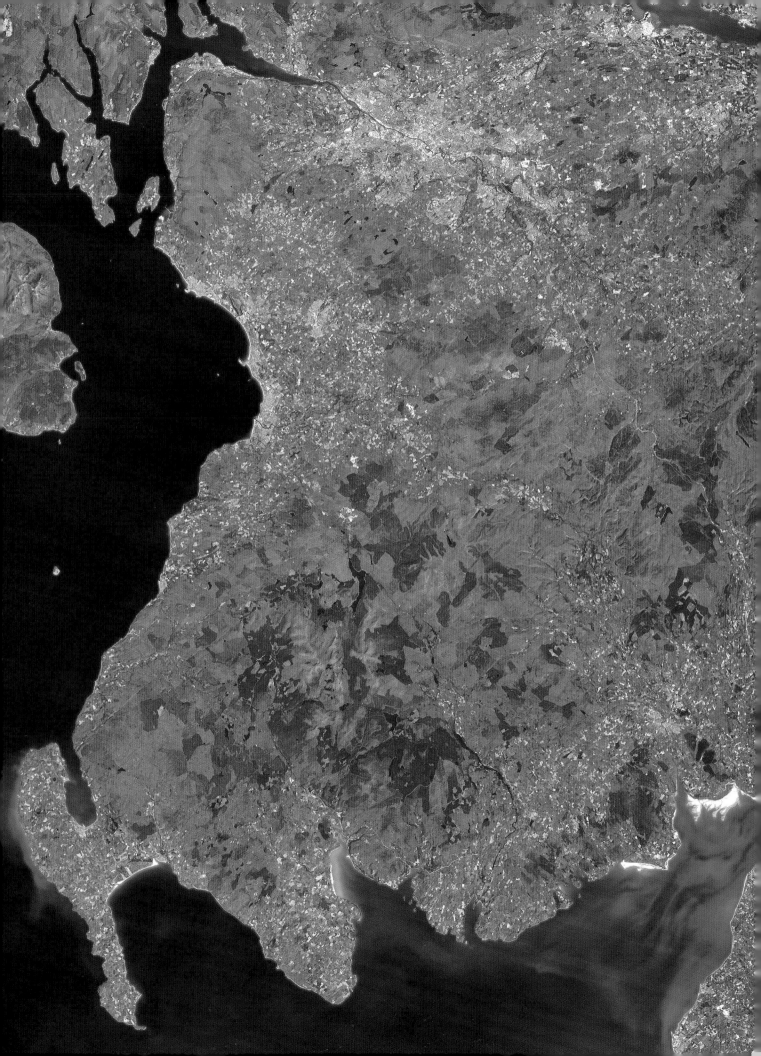

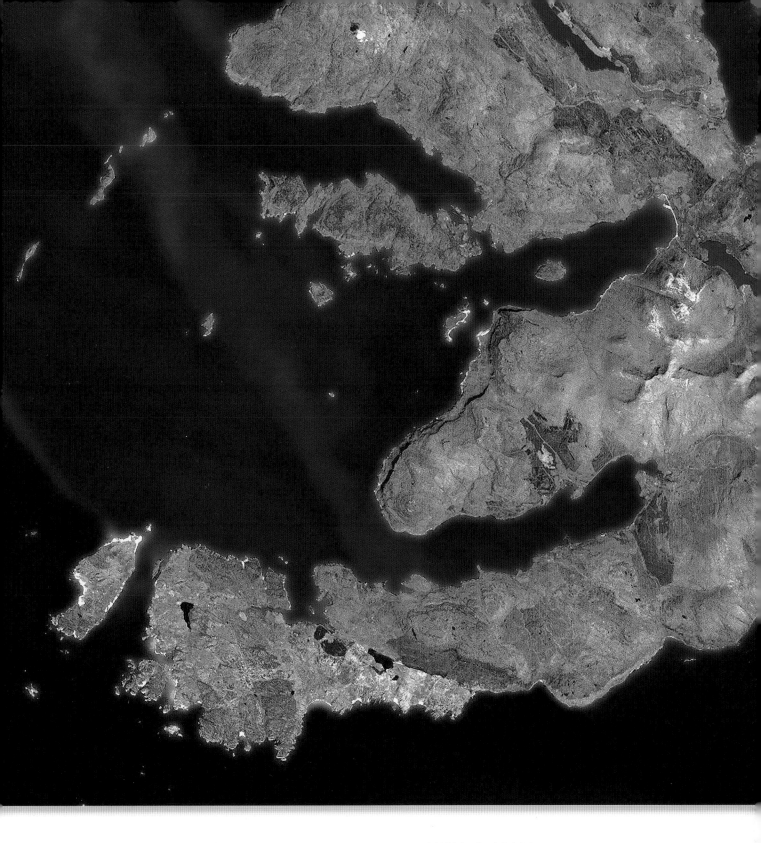

◄ ARGYLL & THE ISLES

The western landscape of Argyll is an indented and complex mixture of mainland and island. Around 100 miles separates the north of Mull from the south of Kintyre, and it is more than 70 miles from Loch Lomond westward to Tiree.

▲ MULL & IONA

Mull's western seaboard is pierced by three large sea lochs: Loch Tuath, Loch na Keal and Loch Scridain in the south. Iona with its sandy beaches lies to the west of the Ross of Mull.

The Scottish coastline stretches for over 7000 miles. There are nearly 800 islands, about 600 of which lie off the West Coast. Only some 10 per cent are inhabited.

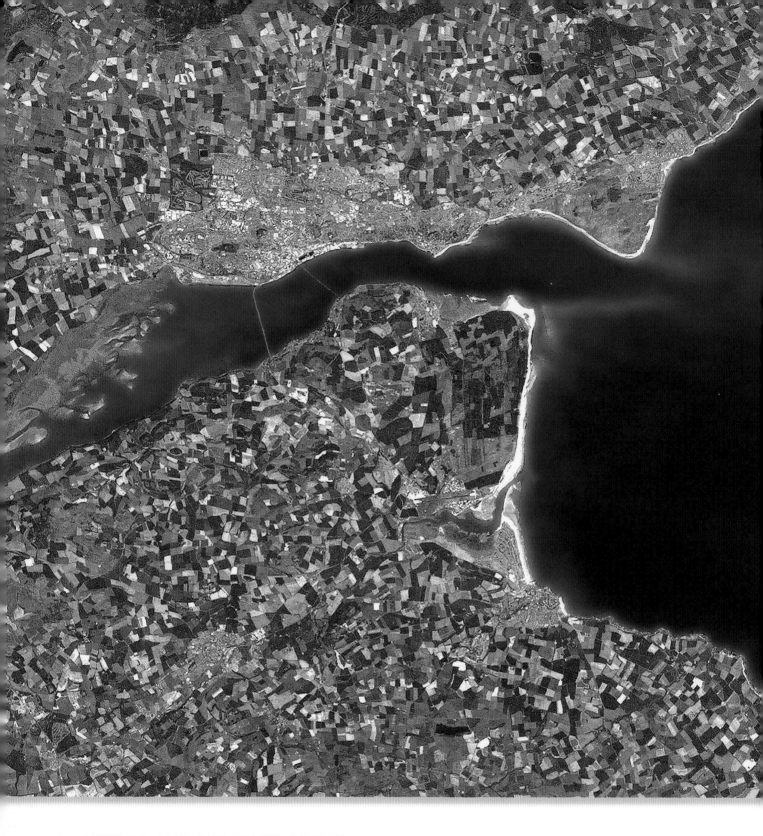

▲ DUNDEE AND THE FIRTH OF TAY

On the triangular headland of Buddon Ness east of Dundee are the golf courses of Carnoustie. St Andrews and its famous links lie to the south of Eden Mouth on the east coast of Fife.

▶ PERTHSHIRE, FIFE AND ANGUS

The fertile lowlands of Fife, Angus and Perthshire run from the Firth of Forth in the south to the clearly defined foothills of the Grampian Mountains in the north.

The Tay river system is the longest in Scotland at 177 miles. The Tay Bridge is the longest railway bridge in the UK at about 2 miles long, and the Tay Road Bridge, completed in 1966, is over 1.4 miles long, just a fraction shorter than the Forth Road Bridge.

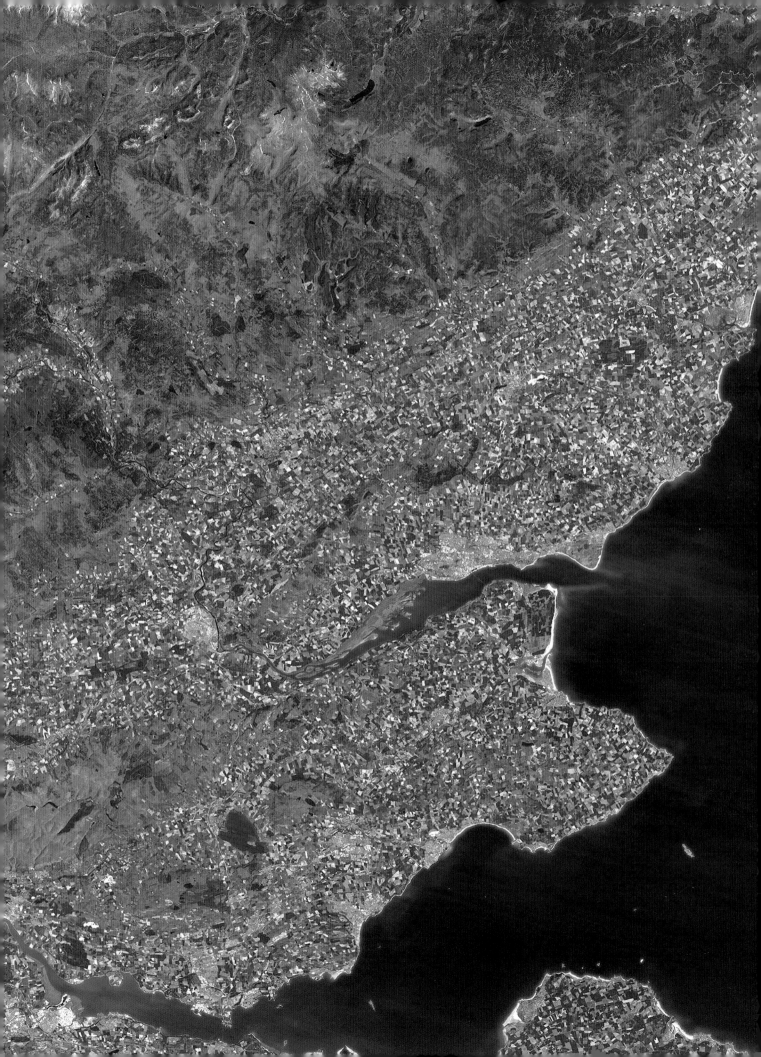

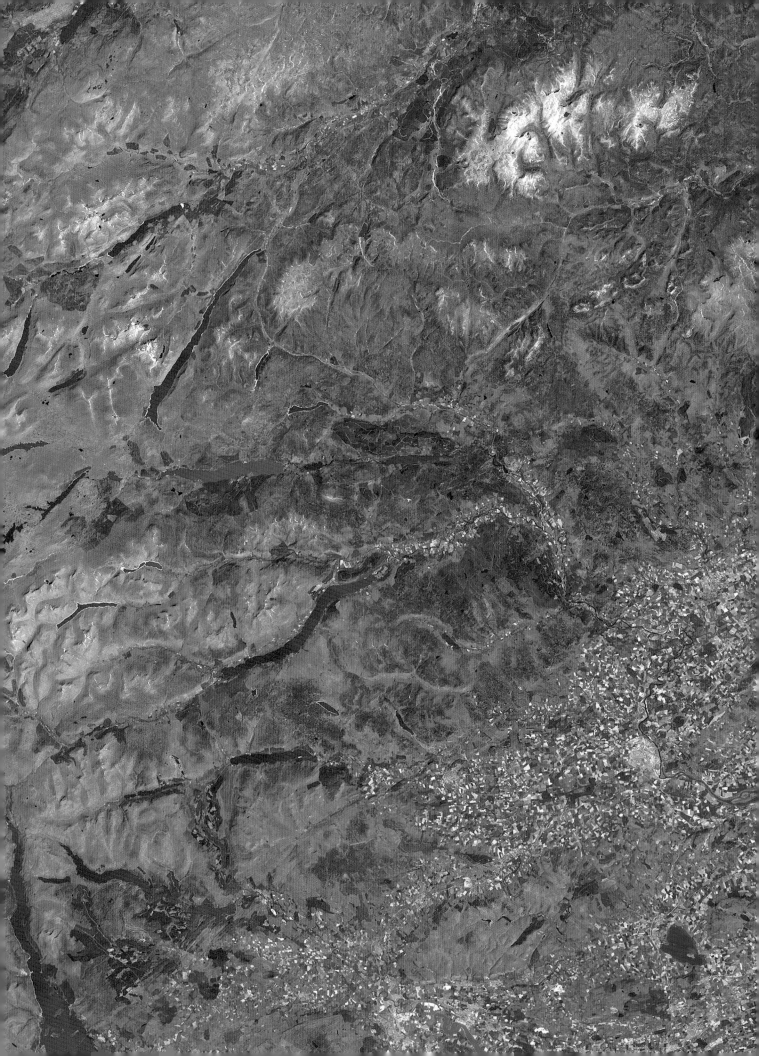

◀ THE CENTRAL HIGHLANDS

Loch Lomond lies to the west of Stirling, the 'gateway to the Highlands'. Northward from Perth, the Grampian Mountains begin to dominate the landscape, culminating in the snow-capped Cairngorms.

▲ THE CAIRNGORM MOUNTAINS

The Cairngorms form Britain's most extensive mountain range and unique sub-Arctic landscape. Its plateau includes five of the country's highest mountains: Ben Macdui, Braeriach, Cairn Toul, Sgor an Lochain Uaine and Cairn Gorm.

The Cairngorms National Park covers an area of 1467 square miles and is Britain's largest national park — 25% of Britain's threatened bird, animal and plant species are found within its boundaries.

▲ THE CITY OF ABERDEEN

The River Don and the River Dee frame the city of Aberdeen, as they flow into the North Sea.

▶ ABERDEENSHIRE & THE NORTHEAST

The northeast coast is ringed with characteristic towns and villages: from Lossiemouth to Fraserburgh in the west, and south from Peterhead to Aberdeen and Montrose.

Scotland's weather is generally cooler than that of the rest of the UK. The west side of the country is wetter and warmer than the east. The coldest temperature recorded in Scotland was -27.2° C on two occasions at Braemar in Aberdeenshire, in 1895 and 1982. The highest temperature of 32.9° C was recorded in August 2003 at Greycrook in the Scottish Borders.

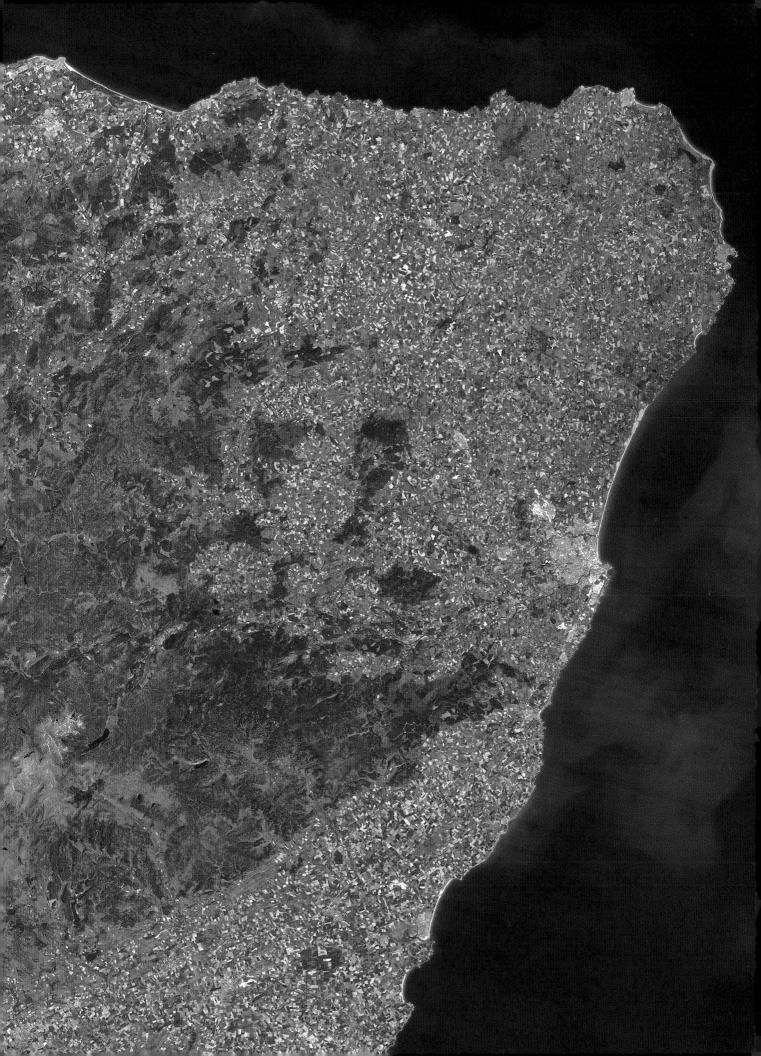

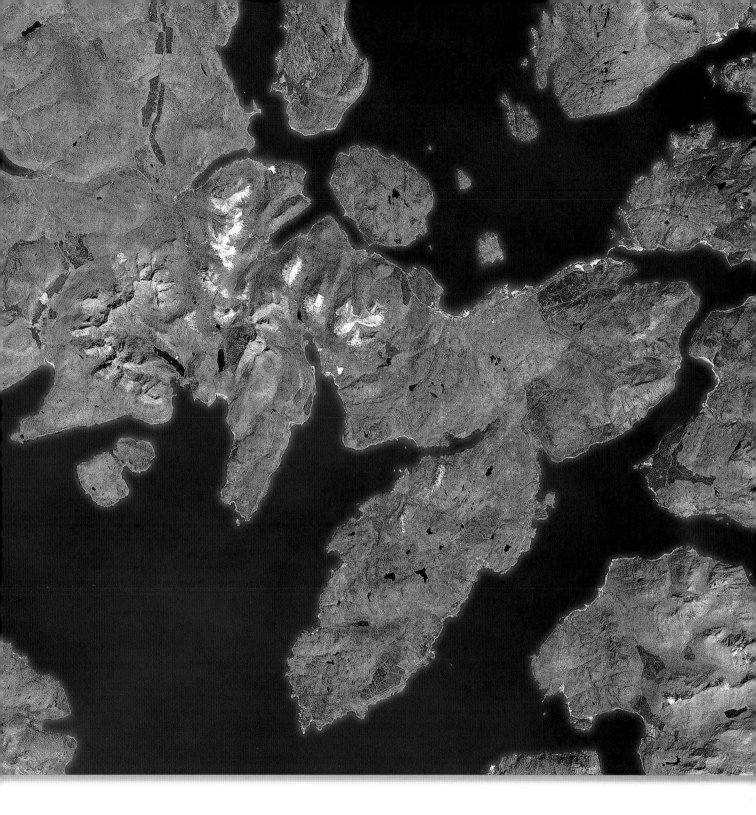

◀ THE NORTHWEST HIGHLANDS

A rugged mountain-and-loch landscape extends from northwest Sutherland down through Wester Ross to Lochaber.

▲ THE ISLAND OF SKYE

The Cuillin Hills dominate central Skye, while in the east, the Skye Bridge links Kyleakin to Kyle of Lochalsh on the mainland.

70% of the total surface area of freshwater in the UK is found in Scotland's 30,000 lochs and 6600 river systems. Loch Lomond is Scotland's largest loch in terms of surface water, with an area of 27.5 square miles and is 24.2 miles long.

▲ SOUTH HARRIS & NORTH UIST

The Sound of Harris separates North Uist from South Harris
and its many long sandy beaches.

▶ THE WESTERN ISLES

The Western Isles feature a mixed landscape of sandy
beaches, machair, blanket peat and huge numbers of lochs.

*The oldest known rock in Britain is Lewisian gneiss, which is more than 3000 million years old,
and forms the foundation of much of the Western Isles, and parts of the northwest Highlands.*

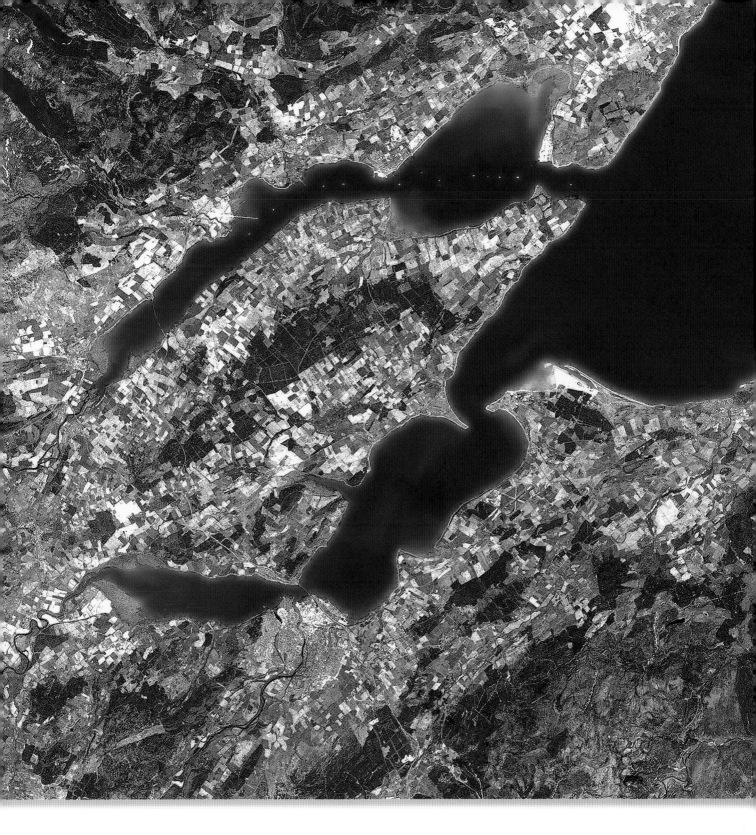

◀ THE HIGHLANDS OF SCOTLAND

The lowland nature of Caithness from Duncansby Head in the east gives way to more rugged Sutherland in the west. To the south lie the Moray Firth, Inverness and Loch Ness.

▲ INVERNESS AND THE BLACK ISLE

The Black Isle is encircled by the Cromarty, Moray and Beauly Firths, and connected to the city of Inverness by the Kessock Bridge.

Loch Ness is part of a geological fault line that runs from Inverness to Fort William.
It holds Scotland's largest volume of water, estimated at over 263,000 million cubic feet, and reaches
a depth of over 700 ft. Loch Morar, at 1017 ft, is the deepest body of fresh water in Europe.

▲ ORKNEY

The islands of Orkney are separated from the mainland by the Pentland Firth. Though most of them are low-lying, many of the islands on the western seaboard have steep cliffs, particularly Hoy.

▶ THE SHETLAND ISLANDS

Shetland, a group of almost 100 islands, is the most northern part of Britain, lying only 200 miles from Norway, and almost 1000 miles from London.

The shortest scheduled flight in the world operates between the islands of Westray and Papa Westray in the Orkney Islands and takes less than two minutes. Scotland's northern latitudes makes winter days short and summer days long. During midsummer in the north of Scotland it does not get completely dark, and Shetland, at 60°00′N, enjoys approximately four hours more daylight than London.

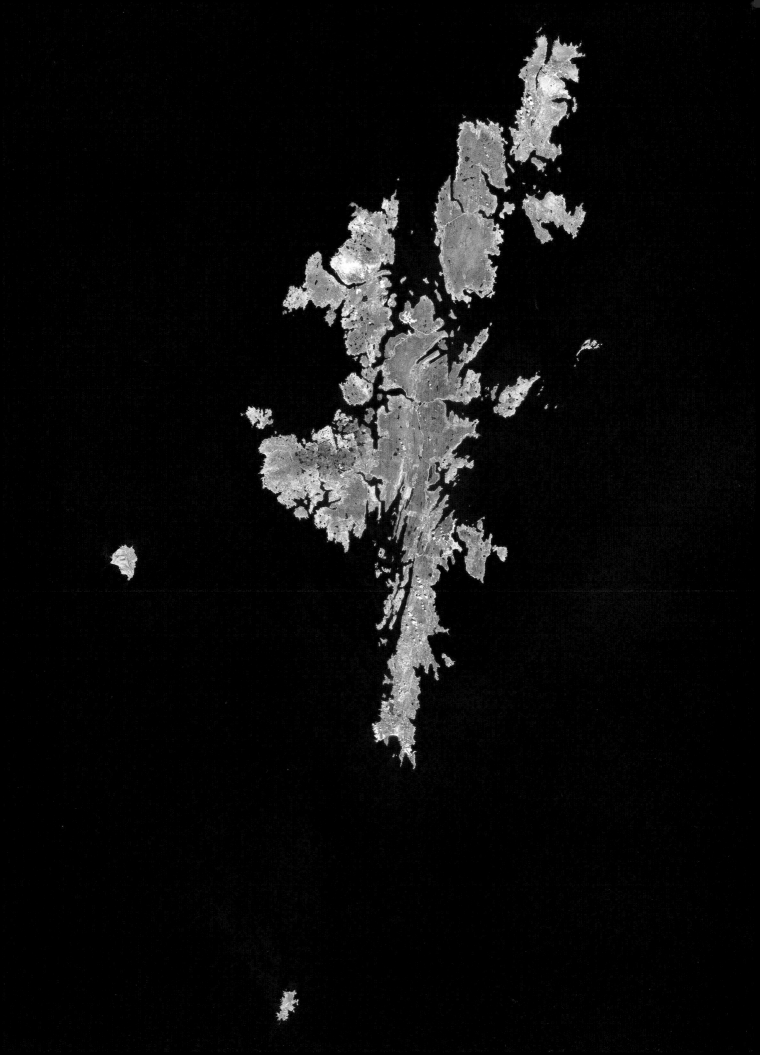

▲ THE FAR NORTH Mountains dominate the landscape of the far northwest, particularly Foinaven, Arkle and Ben Hope.

6000 years ago Scotland's ancient Caledonian Pine Forest covered much of the north of the country. The forest now represents just one per cent of its original range and is spread over 84 small areas, totalling only 65 square miles.

First published in Great Britain in 2006 by
Colin Baxter Photography Limited,
Grantown-on-Spey, PH26 3NA, Scotland

w w w . c o l i n b a x t e r . c o . u k

Photographs copyright © PlanetObserver M SAT www.planetobserver.com

A CIP catalogue record for this book is available from the British Library.

ISBN 1-84107-324-5   978-1-84107-324-8
Printed in China

Front cover picture: Scotland
Page 2 picture: The Firth of Clyde
Back cover picture: Fort William, Ben Nevis & Glencoe